Cool Stuff to Make

hy is this clay so cool? How does it differ from the clay you ordinarily use? For starters, Cool Clay comes in an array of colors. It's easy to handle, doesn't dry out (in case you forget to put it away!), and best of all, when you bake it, the clay hardens. That means you can keep your clay creations forever!

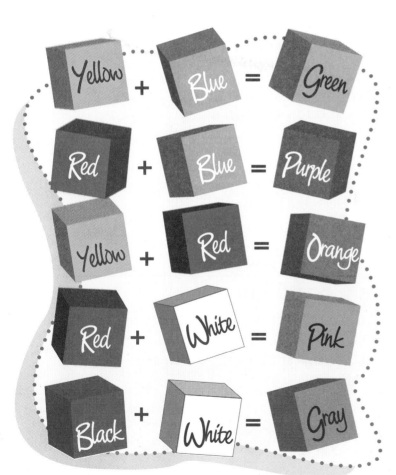

Yellow + Blue = Green

Red + Blue = Purple

Yellow + Red = Orange

Red + White = Pink

Black + White = Gray

Here are some important facts about Cool Clay. Read them carefully. Then turn to a project and begin.

How to Mix Colors

● Mix colors by blending together two or more colors of clay. Use the chart on the left to create the basic colors, but have fun experimenting and creating your own.

Tools to Have Handy

- **Your hands** are the best tools. Be sure to wash them after you've finished handling the clay.

- Use a **sharp knife** for slicing, and only with an adult's permission and supervision.*

- **Toothpicks**, **darning needles**, and **plastic straws** are useful for making different-sized holes in the beads.

- The end of a **pen** is a good tool for pushing and shaping the clay.

- **Waxed paper** makes an easy-to-clean work surface. When you're finished, just throw it away!

- Use a **rolling pin** or an **empty glass bottle** to flatten and smooth clay.*

- With a **ruler** you can measure clay snakes as well as lengths of cord for necklaces and bracelets.

* Keep knife and rolling pin as clay tools only.
Do not use for preparing or eating food.

How to Store Cool Clay

- Cool Clay doesn't dry out, but it does attract lint, dust, cat fur, and just about anything else floating around. To prevent this, store your clay in a plastic container with a lid. A clean margarine tub works well.

How to Bake Cool Clay

● Bake your Cool Clay pieces on an aluminum foil-covered cookie sheet or metal tray. Generally the clay pieces are baked at 275° F (135° C) for 15 minutes in a conventional or toaster oven. NEVER BAKE COOL CLAY IN A MICROWAVE OVEN.

● Since oven temperatures often vary, it's a good idea to test-bake a piece of light-colored clay. If the clay discolors, next time bake it for a shorter period of time. If the clay is not rock hard, however, then bake it for a slightly longer period of time.

● After the clay is baked, use a pot holder to remove the tray from the oven. Be careful not to touch the clay or the tray. The clay will still be soft as well as hot. Let the clay pieces cool for five to ten minutes before lifting them off the tray.

● Remember: Always have an adult's supervision when you bake the clay. If you notice a slight plastic smell while the clay is baking, open a window for ventilation.

Clay Ball Sizes

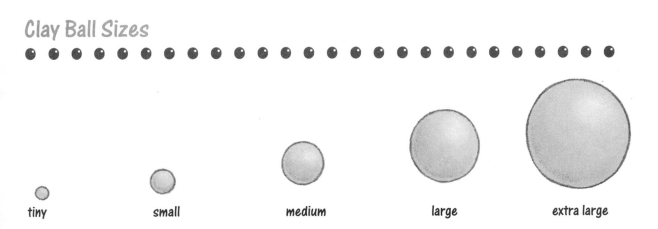

tiny   small   medium   large   extra large

★ If you wish to purchase additional clay, ask for polymer oven-bake clay at arts and crafts stores.

Marvelous Marbleized Beads

Simple and fun to make, these beads are swirls of color.

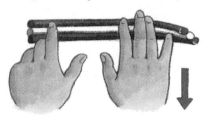  

1. Roll three large balls of clay, each in a different color, into 6"- (15 cm-) long snakes. Place the three snakes next to each other and, holding the ends with your index finger, use your palm to roll the snakes in a downward motion to create a single large snake.

2. Roll the snake into a ball. Then roll it into a snake again. If you would like more swirls, twist and roll it again.

3. Slice off barrel shapes of equal size. Roll the barrels into balls. Use a toothpick to poke a hole through each ball.

4. Bake the beads at 275° F (135°C) for 15 minutes.*

* See page 3 for baking tips.

Marble Hair Ties

String eight to ten beads onto a piece of elastic and knot the ends. Trim the ends of the knot and position one of the beads over the knot.

For another version, string and knot two large beads onto opposite ends of a piece of elastic. Wrap the hair tie around your hair and slip one bead under the other to hold it in place.

Candy-Cane Beads

Colorful candy-cane stripes make for deliciously appealing beads.

You will need:

- 3 different colors of clay
- knife
- toothpick

1. Roll three large balls of clay, each in a different color, into 6"- (15 cm-) long snakes. Place the three snakes next to each other and, holding the ends with your index finger, use your palm to roll the snakes in a downward motion to create a single large snake.

2. Pick up the snake and, using both hands, gently twist it. Then lay the snake down and roll it back and forth with your palms until it is tight and smooth.

3. Place the snake in the refrigerator for five to ten minutes. Then cut barrel-shaped beads off the snake, slicing straight down for a clean cut. Use a toothpick to pierce a hole through each bead.

4. Bake the beads at 275° F (135° C) for 15 minutes.*

* See page 3 for baking tips.

Candy-Cane Necklace

1. Tie a barrel clasp onto a 16" (41 cm) length of nylon string.

2. String the following bead sequence: 12 seed beads, 1 candy-cane bead, until the necklace is the length you want.

3. Knot the end of the string to the other end of the barrel clasp and trim the excess string.

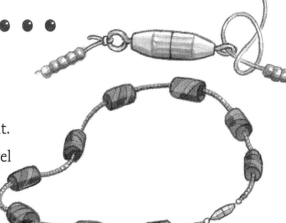

5

Checkerboard Beads

One flip of clay is all it takes to create a stunning checkerboard pattern.

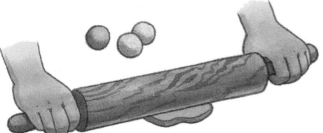

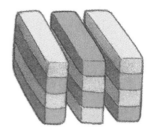

1. Roll two large green balls. Flatten each one by pressing down on it with the side of your fist. Then use your rolling pin to smooth out the clay into thick sheets. Repeat the above procedure with two large yellow balls.

2. Stack these flattened sheets on top of one another, alternating colors. With the rolling pin, lightly smooth out the stack.

3. Cut a square loaf out of the stack. Slice the square into three equal strips. Now flip the center strip over, as shown, and press all three pieces together. Pick up the checkerboard loaf and tap each side on your work surface to pack the design tightly together.

4. Take the red clay and roll an extra-large ball. Flatten it into a sheet with a rolling pin. Wrap this sheet around the checkerboard loaf and trim the edges with your knife. Again pick up the loaf and tap each side on your work surface.

5. Chill the checkerboard loaf in the refrigerator for five to ten minutes for easier slicing. Then slice off the ends and discard. Slice the loaf into beads 1/2" (1 cm) thick or thicker. For each 1/2" (1 cm) bead, poke a hole through the top center. For the thicker beads, run holes through the sides, as shown.

6. Bake the beads at 275° F (135° C) for 15 minutes.*

* See page 3 for baking tips.

Checkerboard Pendant Necklace

• •

Attach a jump ring to a checkerboard bead with a center hole by slightly opening the jump ring with tweezers and inserting the ring through the bead hole. Close the jump ring with tweezers. Onto an 18"- (46 cm-) long black cord, string the checkerboard bead, pony beads, and spacers in a pleasing pattern, keeping the checkerboard bead in the center. Knot together the ends of the cord.

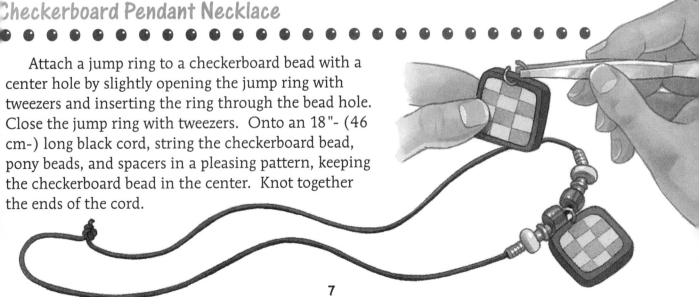

Over the Rainbow Pin

This colorful pin will brighten up your favorite outfit.

You will need:

- clay in a rainbow of colors (red, orange, yellow, green, blue, purple)
- rolling pin
- pencil
- cardboard
- scissors
- knife
- craft glue
- metal pin-backing

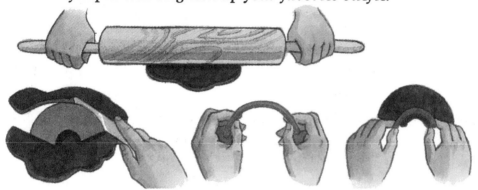

1. Flatten a large ball of any color clay. With a rolling pin, roll the clay into a sheet about 1/4"(.5 cm) thick.

2. Trace the rainbow pattern on this page onto cardboard. Cut out the cardboard pattern and place it on top of the sheet of clay. With a knife, cut around the pattern.

3. Roll red, orange, yellow, green, blue, and purple clay into thin snakes. Curve the snakes into arches and position them onto the clay rainbow shape you cut out in step 2. Gently press each arch into place. Trim off the excess clay.

4. Bake the rainbow at 275° F (135° C) for 15 minutes.*

5. When the rainbow has cooled, use craft glue to glue a metal pin-backing onto the back of the rainbow. Let it dry for several hours.

* See page 3 for baking tips.

pattern

Gingerbread House Magnet

Decorated with candy swirls, candy canes, and gumdrops, this gingerbread house looks yummy enough to eat.

You will need:

- clay in assorted colors
- rolling pin
- toothpick
- knife
- craft glue
- magnet

1. For the house, roll a large ball of brown clay and smooth it out into a sheet about 1/4" (.5 cm) thick. Cut out a square. Use your fingers to smooth out the edges. Make a door from another color of clay. Roll a tiny ball for the doorknob.

2. For the roof, roll out a sheet of white clay and cut out a triangle. Overlap the bottom of the roof with the top of the house. Press down lightly so that the roof adheres to the house. Use your fingers or a knife to make a wavy edge around the bottom of the roof.

3. Roll tiny balls of clay for gumdrops. Make candy canes and swirl candies by rolling two small snakes of different colors. Twist them together and roll them back and forth. Shape them into canes and swirls. Use a toothpick to pick up and place these candies on the house.

4. Bake the gingerbread house at 275° F (135° C) for 15 minutes.*

5. After the house has cooled, glue a magnet on the back of the house with craft glue. Let it dry for several hours.

* See page 3 for baking tips.

Fabulous Fruit

Once you've made these mouthwatering fruits, turn them into fabulous fruit bracelets or earrings.

Strawberry

1. Roll a medium ball of red clay and pinch one end. Tap the round end on your work surface. Use your fingers to shape the clay into a strawberry. With a toothpick, poke shallow holes over the surface.

2. Roll a small ball of green clay and flatten it. Cut out a circle the size of a dime. Cut out tiny triangles to make a star shape and use a toothpick to place it on top of the strawberry. Make a handle by attaching a thin green snake to this top.

Watermelon Slices

Roll a medium green ball and flatten it into a circle. Roll a small red ball and place it on top of the green circle. Press down on it to flatten. Slice the circle in half. Roll tiny black balls for seeds and use a toothpick to place them on the red part of the watermelon.

Orange

Roll a medium orange ball. Use a toothpick to poke shallow holes all the way around.

Apple

Roll a medium red or light green ball. Make a stem by rolling out a thin dark green snake and with a toothpick attaching it to the top of the apple.

If you wish to make beads out of your fruit, first chill the pieces in the refrigerator for about five to ten minutes. Then poke a hole through the center of each fruit piece. Bake the fruit at 275° F (135° C) for 15 minutes.*

* See page 3 for baking tips.

Tutti-Frutti Bracelet

String a variety of fruit beads onto a length of blue cord. Knot the cord after adding each bead. Then tie the ends together.

Watermelon Earrings

To make watermelon earrings, do not poke holes in the fruit before baking. Instead, insert an eye pin into each watermelon slice. Bake at 275° F (135° C) for 15 minutes. When the watermelon slices are cool, attach ear wires to each eye pin.

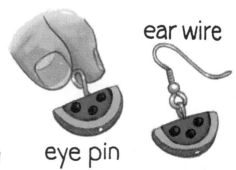

ear wire

eye pin

Heart Pendant

Make this stylish heart pendant for yourself and for a special friend. What a great gift!

1. Roll two large balls of clay in contrasting colors. Flatten these balls and roll them out into rectangular sheets. Trim the rectangles to the same size and stack them.

2. Roll the stacked rectangles into a snake, as shown. Roll the snake until it is pencil thick. Place the snake in the refrigerator for several minutes.

3. In the meantime, roll an extra-large ball from the third clay color. Then take the snake from the refrigerator and cut it into thin slices. Place these slices on the ball. Gently roll the ball between your palms.

4. Mold the ball into a heart shape. With a pencil, pierce a hole through the top center of the heart.

5. Bake the heart at 275°F (135°C) for 15 minutes.*

6. When the heart has cooled, fold the length of cord in half. Thread the folded end through the hole and pull the opposite ends through the loop. Tie the loose ends in a tight knot.

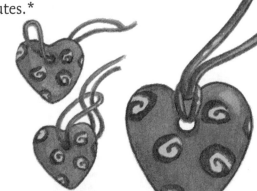

* See page 3 for baking tips.

Snowman Zipper Pull

When you wear this festive zipper pull, you'll feel like you're walking in a winter wonderland.

1. Roll a medium ball of white clay. Roll two more white balls, each a little smaller than the previous one. Place these on top of each other.

2. To make a hat for the snowman, first roll a small ball of black clay. Tap the ends to make a flat top and bottom. Roll the clay back and forth like a wheel. Place the hat on top of the smallest ball of white clay. Roll a thin snake from black clay and wrap it around the bottom of the hat for a brim.

3. Roll five tiny balls of black clay for the snowman's eyes and buttons. Roll a tiny snake from red clay for the mouth and shape a carrot nose from orange clay. Pick up these items with a toothpick and position them on the snowman.

4. Stick the jump ring halfway into the snowman's hat, as shown.

5. Bake the snowman at 275° F (135° C) for 15 minutes.*

6. When the snowman has cooled, attach the snap hook or safety pin to the jump ring. You are now ready to fasten the snowman to a favorite coat or jacket zipper.

*See page 3 for baking tips.

Flower-Power Beads

This eye-popping flower pattern is made by arranging simple snakes into a complex cane.

You will need:

- 3 different colors of clay (for example, yellow, blue, green)
- rolling pin
- sharp knife
- toothpick

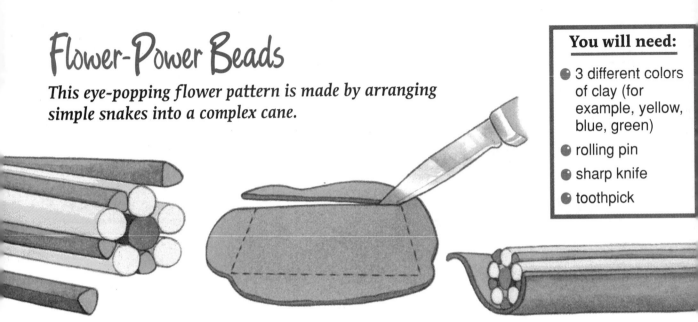

1. Roll five large yellow balls into 6"- (15 cm-) long snakes. Roll a large blue ball into a 6"- (15 cm-) long snake. Press the yellow snakes around the blue one.

2. Make five green triangular logs 6"- (15 cm-) long. Place them in the spaces between the yellow snakes, as shown. Gently roll the stacked snake back and forth.

3. Flatten an extra-large green ball. Use a rolling pin to smooth the clay into a sheet. Cut out a rectangle large enough to wrap once around the snake. Wrap the sheet around the snake. Smooth the joint where the ends meet and trim any extra clay. You now have made a cane.

4. Gently roll the cane back and forth with your palm until the cane is the size you want.* Don't worry about ruining your design as you roll; it will stay the same but reduce in size.

* The size of the cane depends on the project.

14

5. Place the cane in the refrigerator for a few minutes. Then slice the cane into 1/2" (1 cm) beads. Gently roll the beads back and forth like a wheel to even them out. Use your fingers to smooth the surface.

6. Poke holes through the clay, as shown.

7. Bake the beads at 275° F (135° C) for 15 minutes.*

* See page 3 for baking tips.

Flower-Power Barrette

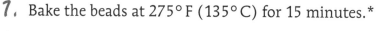

Make this barrette by following steps 1-5 above. Then continue with the instructions listed below.

1. Cover the top of a metal barrette with a band of green clay.

2. Press five or six thin slices from the cane onto the green clay.

3. Place the barrette on a metal tray and bake at 275° F (135° C) for 15 minutes.* Allow the barrette to cool before touching it.

* See page 3 for baking tips.

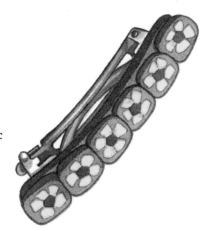

Treasure Tin

Protect your most cherished keepsakes in a treasure tin you've made yourself.

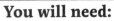

You will need:

● clay in assorted colors

● small, circular, metal tin with lid (such as the kind that contains candy)

Do not substitute a plastic lid.

1. Roll eight to ten medium balls of clay in a variety of colors. Roll each ball into a snake and coil it around itself, as shown.

2. Place some of the coils around the edge of the lid. Then fill in the center of the lid with the rest.

3. Roll small balls in a variety of colors. Place the balls into any gaps that exist between the coils.

4. Roll two large balls of any color clay into snakes. Press these snakes around the side of the lid.

5. Bake the lid for 15 to 18 minutes at 275° F (135°C).* Make sure the lid is completely cool before touching it or placing it on top of the tin.

* See page 3 for baking tips.